Living A Meditative

Lifestyle

LINDA HANNAH YOUNG MA

SWEETSPIRE LITERATURE
——— MANAGEMENT ———

Dedicated to

Greg

Jessica & Calem,

Sarah & Jeffrey

Elijah, Alannah, Zaliah

Kenzi.

Table of Contents

What is unique about you?

Name it and celebrate it!

Color & Diversity

Color upon color, making a
mosaic fabric of beauty.
Appreciate diversity for the
individual expression that it is.
We don't need to make everyone like us.
We are just as we should be, and
we are not the same as
everyone else.

A Labyrinth - Unknown location

Expect twists and turns in life.
They are to be an expected as
part of the journey.

Honoring Your Path

It is the texture and the color that
make the fabric exquisite.

No one knows the course that their life will take;
what twists and turns lie ahead.

All we can do is
honor the path.
Bclieve that in the end,
we will be more enriched and whole
because we chose not to fight it, but
to go with its twists and turns.

Woodend, Victoria

Beautiful or Painful?

You decide.

Changing Perspective

Sometimes the sharpness of life can be harsh.

It can feel unapproachable, uninviting,

or even dangerous.

Take a step back.

What if there is beauty to be

discovered in the pointiness?

What if there is purpose in its approach?

What if there is more to experience

than what you perceive?

Smile, nod, offer a random act of kindness

Step back to gain a new perspective.

It's worth a try.

Garden, Woodend

Pick something out of a garden.

Reflect upon it; its color, shape, smell, texture.

Give thanks.

What are You Looking for?

Your yearning?
Your passion?
Your heart-song?

Look for it today... find it.
Whatever 'it' may be...
Cherish it, honor it.
Give thanks for it.
Hold it lightly and watch it keep
recurring in your life.

Lavender

Stop and smell the lavender!

Look Around You

Look not only to the things in the
foreground of your life.

There are equally magical occurrances
happening in the background too.

For millions of years before you, the tide came in
and went out again.
For millions of years after you, the tide
will come in and go out again.
Lighten up and enjoy all of life!

Melbourne, Australia

How can you be more gentle
with yourself?

Sometimes Life Can Be...

Messy

Disorganised

Lacking Vision

Unnavigable

Guess What?

Chaos can turn into Creation!

Slowly

Intentional Small Steps

Gently Does It

Easy as She Goes

Bit by Bit

You Can Do It!

Torquay, Victoria

Make a decision and choose
the best way for you.
Over, Under, Sit for a while?

Bridges or Walls?

One person's bridge is another person's wall.
The trick is to accept it for what it is,
admire it and move accordingly.

Go around, jump over, dig under,
turn away.
You get to choose!

Woodend, Victoria

Find a safe place outside to lie down
And look at the sky.
Watch the clouds.
You are a part of this story of creation.

The Journey of Clouds

Clouds morph and change.
Sometimes dark and
full of rain,
Sometimes
light and wispy.
Life morphs and changes.
Sometimes dark and
full of despair,
Sometimes light and full of joy.
All have purpose in the
scheme of things.
Everything is ever moving
and morphing.
Allow despair to pass through your
life just as the clouds do.

Torquay, Victoria

What do you need more of?

What do you need less of?

Balance

Balance is the answer:
A little of this, a little bit of that, a little work,
a little play, a little ocean, a little sand.

A little of what is good for you and
brings balance and harmony.

Where Do You
Need
Balance
In
Your Life?

The Great Ocean Road, Victoria

What do you need to let go of?

The Swells of Life

Make the most of the swell and notice
the good that is in it.

Ride it, Jump it,
Surf it, Play in it.

But don't let it overcome you.
Respect the nature of things.
Whatever your situation, it will resolve.
It always does, eventually!

Pure As A Flower

Precious one,
let go of your pain,
your hurts, your anguish.
Acknowledge it.
Cry, scream, roll up in a ball if
you need to, for a time.
Then give it permission
to leave you.
Love is as pure as a flower – ready to be
picked and to be given to another.

Let go!
Let God.

Woodend, Victoria

Think of the cycle of a rose.

A lifeless looking, dead bush.

Slowly nodes appear on the stems.

Eventually green shoots appear.

Leaves grow, buds appear,

Beautiful blooms come for a time.

They whither as do the leaves.

A lifeless looking, dead bush remains.

Where are you in the cycle of growth

or dormancy in your life?

Location Unknown

What was your last surprise?

How did it affect you?

Surprise!

Look for the unexpected, the flash of color in
a green field, a flock of birds in the blue sky.

There is gift in the *Surprise*!

Accept each unexpected occurrence
as a kiss from the Creator, wrapped
in nature, sent with love.

The Great Ocean Road, Victoria

Imagine being carried in your despair.
Give thanks to the one who carries you.

Trust

Trust that you are being carried
through rough times.
You are being carried; the footprints
of the one who carries you are strong,
stable and able to carry you through all
manner of isolation and desperation.

Trust.

Halls Gap, Victoria

Search for the hope that maybe hidden.

Growth in Desolation

Impenetrable

Severe

Homeless

...but is it?

Even in the harshness of life's

challenges there are

hints of hope and

splashes of newness

Search for it!

Melbourne, Australia

Who is precious in your life?

Do they know that to be true for you?

It might be time to share it with them.

Precious

As the dew falls to the ground
And sprinkles nourishment
All around,
God's love for you
Can be found.
In every sight
And every sound.

You are
Loved
Cherished
Precious

Marysville, Victoria. Cover Photo Pre-bushfire

This photo was taken in Marysville, Victoria in 2006. A few years later in 2009 the whole region was devastated by a life-taking bushfire. 173 souls lost, 2029 homes gone, 2796 square miles devastated, uncountable numbers of Animals lost.

Regeneration has now returned; not the same, but different.

Ever Changing

Nothing stays the same.
Everything is in cyclic patterns of newness,
growth, deconstruction, death.

But death is not the end.
It makes way for the next unknown phase;
not the same,
but different.

Give and Take

Life gives and takes away
and gives again.
It's all in the waiting for a new
but different reality to appear.
Creation is always there waiting for you,
inviting you to join in with its calming rhythm.
It's inviting you to slow down, breathe deeply
and allow its healing flow to touch you.
You owe it to yourself and to the world to allow
it to blossom within you and around you.

Mt. St. Helens, Washington

When did you last spend time in nature?

Howl It Out

Let your true self howl your song
from the mountain tops.
Let yourself experience love and give love.

Let yourself receive gratitude and give gratitude.

Because you are loved from the highest
peaks to the lowest depths of the ocean.
You are a precious creation...
You are unique and individual...
You are blessed...
Sing it out...

Howl it from your soul...
Declare the uniqueness of others.
Declare that they too are blessed.
It's written in the earth's DNA!

Alberta, Canada

Howl with joy!
You are alive!

Metcalf, Victoria

What can you encourage today?

Nourish Your Heart Song

Just as the river's flow, brings life
to its surrounding areas...

So too are you to bring life and light
to all that you touch in your day.

May your Heart-Song bring nourishment,
encouragement and growth to all
those you meet each day.

Venice Beach, California

How can you celebrate diversity today?

Beauty in Diversity

I love diversity.
I love variation.
I love different environments and habitats.
I love contrast and color.
I love texture and fragrance.
I love beautiful tones and shades in skin color.

Why do we criticise difference?
Why are wars fought over diversity?
Why do we judge?

Beauty in diversity and difference.
As God made it!

Seeds of Love

One seed can multiply into millions of plants.

One seed of kindness could expand
and travel around the globe.

One seed of honesty could stop all the wars.

One seed of love could make us realise
we are all sisters and brothers on
this same journey called life.

Buninyong, Victoria

What seeds will
you plant today?

There's Only One You

Of all the people who have ever
been and will ever be,
there is only one you.

So spread your wings and fly.

Don't be content with what others
think you can or cannot do.

Only you have the potential to be
the best you.

This is your time.
Be Authentically You!

Colorado, USA

How can you express your uniqueness today?

(P.S. No one else can do it, but you!)

Unique

Everything is unique and has its own
contribution to make to the world.
If one chooses not to contribute, the
world is less because of that decision.

Choose to participate;
sing out your unique gifts and
reveal the Divine in your soul
to the world.

Tell someone today what unique part of their
personality you admire.
It will be a gift for them.

What is your Heart-Song?

Describe it, reflect on it, own it.

Look to Nature

Look to nature and allow it to
be a blessing to you.
As you do you will be empowered to bless others.
Just as a flower's beauty speaks to our soul,
so the beauty that we emanate will speak to
the soul of another.
You are the light of the world.
(Mat 5:14)

Your Heart-Song is the rhythm
of the world.
Sing it, play it, influence for good
and watch the magic happen.

Share Your Uniqueness

It's true!

We are all here for each other.

The more we give,

the more we will get.

The more you love,

The more you will receive love.

It's as simple and as

complicated as that!

There is a purpose for everything.

Woodend, Victoria

What is your purpose?

What fires you up and inspires you?

What brings you joy?

Whatever it is,

That is what you are here to share.

A Beach, East Coast Australia

Seek and you shall find.

Knock and the door will be open.

(Matthew 7:7)

Treasure in the Trash

Find the good within the bad.

Find the treasure within the trash.

Find the lesson within the test.

Find the joy within the sadness.

Even if it is small, it is there for the looking.

Ventnor, Victoria

What do you need to be who authentically are?

It Is What It Is!

Some things in life seem
insurmountable and maybe
they are.
It's alright.
Appreciate it for what it is.
There is another path
to take.

Don't fight it.
It is what it is, and you are
who you are.
Acknowledge the challenges.
You are in the process
of change!

About the Author

Linda (Hannah) Young

B.Teach., B.Ed., B.Theol., M.A.,GDipSup., D.Min(candidate)

Born: 1962 Australia

Studied in:

Education

Theology

Spirituality

Coaching

Supervision

Doctorate in Ministry (Candidate)

Passions:

Family & Friends | Creativity | Music | Art

Home Making

French

Travelling

Other Publications:

A Note for Children – Book, CD, MP3

Living in Abundance – Co-Author

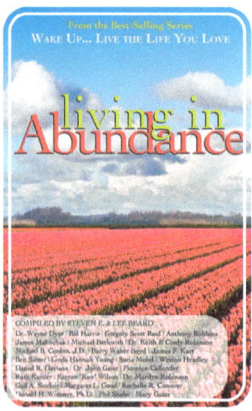

In the Spirit of Success – Co-Author

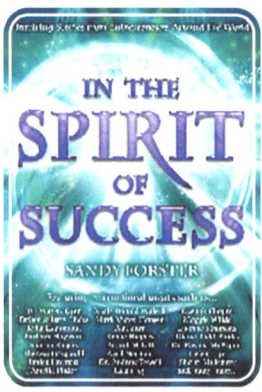

All publications can be found on Amazon

Acknowledgements

Reflections by:
Linda Hannah Young MA

Photographs by:
Linda Hannah Young
Gregory Young
All photographs were taken
in Australia or North America
Deeply Implicit©2023

www.ingramcontent.com/pod-product-compliance
Lightning Source LLC
Chambersburg PA
CBHW041552120626
46551CB00002B/183